T0350606

WHEN THE BLUE GOES

The Poems of Robert Nash

Translated from the French by
Françoise Besnard Canter

Down East Books

Down East Books

An imprint of Globe Pequot
Trade division of The Rowman & Littlefield Publishing Group, Inc.
4501 Forbes Blvd., Ste. 200
Lanham, MD 20706
www.rowman.com
www.downeastbooks.com

Distributed by NATIONAL BOOK NETWORK

Library of Congress Cataloging-in-Publication Data

Names: Nash, Robert, 1930-1995?, author. | Besnard Canter, Françoise, translator. | Nash, Robert, 1930-1995? Maine. English. | Nash, Robert, 1930-1995? Poèmes à un ami français. English. | Nash, Robert, 1930-1995? Poèmes épars dans une chemise en carton vert. English.
Title: When the blue goes : the poems of Robert Nash / translated from the French by Françoise Besnard Canter.
Description: Lanham, MD : Down East Books, 2022. | Poems originally written in French and published in France in three separate volumes, translated into English. | Summary: "Newly discovered work by a previously unknown Maine poet "-- Provided by publisher.
Identifiers: LCCN 2022007830 (print) | LCCN 2022007831 (ebook) | ISBN 9781684750429 (cloth) | ISBN 9781684750436 (ebook)
Subjects: LCSH: Nash, Robert, 1930-1995?--Translations into English. | LCGFT: Poetry.
Classification: LCC PQ3939.N37 W47 2022 (print) | LCC PQ3939.N37 (ebook) | DDC 841/.914--dc23/eng/20220217
LC record available at https://lccn.loc.gov/2022007830
LC ebook record available at https://lccn.loc.gov/2022007831

For Robert Tardif

Contents

Preface

Life is conducive to encounters, and these are often stronger when unexpected. Such was my encounter with Robert Nash. A man, a poet, I once knew nothing about and who now seems so close to me. I discovered Nash in a mass of trunks and boxes, more precisely when I opened one of them. Here he was! Lost among papers and photographs, in stacks of scattered pages. Many were wrinkled, torn, stained, unreadable. Dust and humidity, the enemies of memory, had started to harm and altogether erase him, with the help of other allies—learned rodents seeing an opportunity for more erudition.

In fact, I must confess that I was looking for something other than poetry in the basement of the family house. It is, nevertheless, poetry that I found! I remember trying to decipher one first text, then others—a little surprised to begin with, then astonished. The writer was addressing my father, calling him *"mon ami"* (my friend). He was giving him news, not in an epistolary form, but rather in the form of poems. He used no artifice at all, writing sometimes in his language (English), sometimes in the language of my father (French), and apologizing often for speaking it *"si mauvais"* (so poorly). No rhetorical effects altered his words and, despite the passing of time and the fact that I was not the one to whom these texts were addressed, it seemed he spoke directly to me. I tried to imagine the man, Robert Nash, and especially his friendship with my father. With my fingers, I delved through the stacks of papers I would soon call "his archives." Some pages would crumble, tear, or even fall into pieces. It was a child's game, a treasure hunt, and the object of this hunt a shred of memory. Digging into the past, I discovered glimpses of lives and I re-discovered my father, a facet of him I did not know. I excavated papers covered with dense handwriting half-erased: bits of sentences, crumbs of words, not fully faded—and so moving.

I became almost frantic, opening boxes and folders in hope of uncovering yet another poem-letter from Nash. I was both excited and distraught. Nothing for a while and then, suddenly, the writing would appear, wrecked by the years, by the oblivion in which it had been steeped and aged. Sometimes the writing persisted and the struggle to stay alive resonated in me like a call. What should I do?

I could not let these texts literally rot. I found them necessary because of their earnestness. They evoke a man who speaks of life, death, love, and friendship with a solemn simplicity and an emotion that enlarges their scope. In speaking to his friend, he was speaking to all of us. His words were holding me there, in this basement lit only by a small window and a simple light bulb. That is why I am offering you these texts (out of many unusable or lost). These are the poems I could rescue. I hope I have respected, if not exactly the letter, at least the spirit of what I call, with no hesitation, the poetry of Robert Nash.

—Jean Claude Tardif

Introduction

Translating Robert Nash—An Unusual Adventure

In the spring of 2017, Jean-Claude Tardif, a poet, a writer, and the editor of the French poetry revue, *À l'index*, e-mailed me a few poems by a Robert Nash along with these enigmatic lines: "As I was cleaning the basement of my parents' house in Brittany, I found these old papers in a trunk. I realized they were poems mainly in French sent to my father (who didn't speak English) by an American friend. These poems reflect forty years of friendship between the two men. If you like them, would you like to translate them into English?"

The depth of Robert Nash's poems, his profound solitude and his intimate and healing relationship with nature immediately moved me. Right away I found myself swept into the sorrow of a man who has lost everything and has only his words left. I was also intrigued by the story of the poems' discovery and by the lifelong friendship between Nash and Jean-Claude's father. I wanted to know more. However, aside from what emerges from the poems, so little of him is known. The mystery captivated me and stimulated in me a strong desire to follow in Nash's footsteps, to embark on the unique, almost musical, experience of re-composing his voice. But how? This was new to me. I write poems both in French and English, and I translate them from one language to the other, but here, I had to revive a voice that was not mine. I took the challenge to heart and embarked with Jean

Claude on this incredible journey, which gave birth within five years to three bilingual volumes published in France: *Maine, Poems to a French Friend*, and *Scattered Poems Gathered in a Green Folder*. These three volumes are now combined, in the order of their original publication, into this U.S. edition, *When the Blue Goes*.

With each collection, new pieces of the puzzle of Nash's life come to light. It is important to note that the three collections do not follow Nash's life in a chronological order but rather the order in which Jean-Claude discovered the poems in the old house. From *Maine*, the first series of poems Jean-Claude found, we understand that Nash's family emigrated from Sussex when he was a child, that his son Lee died in Vietnam in 1974, and his wife Catriona two years later. It is also in this first collection that we learn of Nash's disappearance in May of 1995, just a week after he wrote his last dated poem.

Poems to a French Friend tells us that Nash and Jean-Claude's father, who shared the same (very common at the time) first name Robert, met in the north of France in the early fifties and that Nash and his family lived in Delaware. We also see that both Nash and his wife Catriona were fluent in French and that it was Catriona who had originally wanted to move to Maine, a wish fulfilled by Nash after her death.

In *Poems Gathered in a Green Folder*, we meet his faithful friends from Maine: Ours Bleu, the Algonquin, who rescues him when he is sick, feeds him, and interprets his dreams; Randall, who comes to repair his old Chevrolet; Emerson, the badger*, his silent companion from the early days, the fox, the racoon, and Jack Brent, the last-mentioned friend in this collection. With each poem, new questions emerged, enlarging the scope of what has become a never-ending mystery.

At the end of my first adventure with Robert Nash, as I was writing the forward to the first bilingual volume, I promised myself I would go to Maine to explore the landscape and to discover something of the voice that had lived with me for more than a year. In April 2019, my friend Sarah Porter and I went to Augusta in the footsteps of our friend. With the help of librarian Julie Olson, we organized a reading at the Lithgow Library, and we tried, while in town, to find tangible traces of Nash's existence. We went to City Hall to see if there were any record of the purchase of land or property in the early eighties by a Robert Nash. We went to the oldest hardware store in town, most likely the one mentioned in Nash's poems. We Googled "Robert Nash" to see if he had published anywhere. We even tried to find his son's name on the official list of soldiers who had died or were reported lost in Vietnam. We found nothing. I knew then that what we know and will continue to discover of Robert Nash will only come from his words. As a poet and translator, my curiosity stops here. Robert Nash's voice in his poetry is enough for me.

My journey with Nash transformed me. He became my friend. I walked with him in the intimacy of the Maine woods. I felt the light and the brisk winds of spring. I climbed Maine's mountains. I followed the flights of osprey and wild geese. I saw the clawed tracks of a badger. I met the light-gray eyes of Catriona and felt the sorrow of a mother and father who have lost their son, and I got closer and closer to the poet, his death becoming more present with each new poem until the last. Sometimes, I catch myself reciting bits of poems as if they were mine. The metamorphosis Nash's words offered me is now an intrinsic part of my writing. I became Nash.

Nash's evocations, observations, and silences linger in my thoughts long after their translation. They bring purpose and joy to many of my days. During these past years of confinement and political turmoil, I found solace in reviving his words. Ultimately, I know that the woods of Maine, with their trees and wild animals, were for the bereaved Nash, a place of solitude, a place of friendship, a place of healing and a home for his poems. *When the Blue Goes* is the fulfilment of my journey with Robert Nash. I hope to transmit to every reader who enters Nash's poetry the pleasure and the magic languages sometimes accomplish.

—Françoise Besnard Canter

* *Author's Note: While badgers are not typically found in Maine, and Nash may well have been speaking about a different animal, he chose his words carefully, so we've preserved his use of the word in these translations.*

Acknowledgments

I want to thank Jean Claude Tardif for giving me the gift of Robert Nash.

I also want to thank my friends Faiza El Solh and Sarah Porter, who helped refine the final versions of the English translations and accompanied me on this journey from the very beginning.

Finally, I want to express my deep gratitude to Michael Steere and Down East Books for recognizing the unique value of Robert Nash's poetry and for providing his poetry a readership in English.

Maine

The Indian

I look at the old Indian who walks in the street
paying no attention to traffic.
His skin wears the color of a soil
no longer his.
I look at him.
With L'Œuvre au noir* tucked under my arm,
I walk up toward the university.
I think of my son
dead near a river, somewhere, over there,
in Vietnam.
I look at the Indian,
at the dust raised with each
of his very old steps
on this soil no longer his.
We are roughly the same age.
But he, who does he think about?
How many lost sons, lost souls
mixed with his soil,
and weary dreams?

* The Abyss, *by Marguerite Yourcenar*

In this village, I have spent all my years,
my nights, my days, and their in-betweens.
People die and live here,
like everywhere else.
They greet each other
convinced they do something other
than live and die.
The sound of the ocean enters,
a curious unexpected neighbor,
a boisterous unruly child
leaving salty smells on windshields
and traces of the distant nights
and indifferent days
remembered in silence
as one thinks of lost friends.

When I look through the window,
I imagine the vast forests edged with colors
and shadows on the other side of the border,
the moving autumns and
transparent winters of New Brunswick—
memories my friend Old Falcon, the Algonquin,
would often speak of
in front of a plate of pink clams.
He would tell me of moose
and wolf tracks from his childhood
when his grandfather made them
come alive with words
and when the swirling weight of a maple leaf in September
would announce the presence of the world
better than any television news.

Today
my friend weighs the weight of a red leaf
the wind is blowing against the window.
I think of him
every day
since his last hunt
his last dream.
Tomorrow, for sure!
I shall leave for the South Twin Lake.
I shall bring along the bare minimum
plus a book,
the antidote to the weight of my tears.

Sometimes the blue of the ocean
in the smallest creek
lost in the eyes of my wife
mirrors the islands
the color of the rocks
the uncertain shades of seasons
the long-lashed eyes of deer
we hunt
in search of beauty
behind the lens of a camera.

When the blue goes away
I read French authors
for no reason
for the sole pleasure of the black ink
on a white page
lit by a storm lantern.
I think of the whirling sparks of lighthouses.
Sometimes a sparrow
lands on the
porch railing.
Did it cross the border?
Does it sing in Acadian?
I wait.
I feel its weariness respond to mine
silence is our common good.

This morning in Augusta's streets
I feel far from home.
In the window of a bookstore
a book on the traditions of the Wabanaki people
sits next to a history by Samuel de Champlain
and a manual on fishing techniques
in the Grand Banks of Newfoundland.
How long did I stay there
staring at those book covers
trying to forget
the noise and the smell of the city?

Last night, big fuss around the house
as if the night were trying to enter,
but no wind in the trees
autumn is at rest
and the ocean is too far to worry about,
roaring like a wounded bear
trapped in the strength of its rage,
nevertheless
big fuss around the house.
Under its belly
the earth snuggles up
afraid of being hurt
of becoming more red than usual.
I listen to her, listen to them:
the night, the ocean, the trees, the bear, the wounded soil,
and I know they do not listen.
With daylight,
I discover on the porch steps,
a few tufts of fur, a few traces of blood
and, in the soft soil,
the clawed tracks of a badger.

Another day looking outside,
filling my eyes with the flight of an osprey,
waiting for the first snows.
I think of Thoreau,
of his words, with their scent of the forest,
of maples and conifers.
And I think of South Twin Lake,
which I shall see, another time, with the light
and soft winds of spring.
This morning, I see the tracks of a badger
on the trail, near the wood pile.
It had been weeks since it came for a visit.
Its left foreleg is wounded
one claw left no imprint on the wet ground.
No doubt, a younger one from the clan.
Time goes by, steadily,
till death.

To take the Appalachian trail
at the crack of dawn
and to walk until nightfall
as if crossing the threshold of a sugar shack
or that of a church
leaving the door open
to invite the wind
to welcome all the elements
as if it were the last time
and to breathe deeply
to be sure to be alive.

Fields of cornflowers
her eyes, long gone,
shivers of the moving blue,
her eyelashes in the morning light
gold dust, comet's tail,
scents of the last dream before waking,
Catriona smiles at me!
I remember
as I remember the smell of waves
the foam, the flight of sea birds.
Fields of cornflowers, here,
to not forget that the forgotten is
sometimes
all that remains.

All day long the noise of the saw
cuts the big silence that surrounds me.
Under my shirt the muscles sweat and
the blood flows hard and red
so that I can still make it through another day
and breathe until evening
and gnaw the dark bone of night
yet another time
without being sated.

Sometimes I see Lee's face
I hear his voice and Catriona's singing her little songs
I try to sing along with them
but nothing comes.
Nothing from my mouth but silence
my lips are dry
my eyes wet from the effort
to remember.
Yesterday, in Augusta,
I tried to talk with Ed, the doctor.
He told me that he sees nothing wrong.
With age,
swallowing becomes harder.

Tonight again around the fire
sparks, the crackling wood
shadows and smell of sap
on the flat stones
nestled in the earth.
I look at the stars
the North Star
whose light comes
from so far
until it is reflected in my eyes.
I follow the clouds, the light shadows
playing hide and seek in the tree-tops.
I am so far away!
and yet, still here
in my dreams and childhood fears.

Sometimes I remember.
I see her telling him the story of Norumbega,
the men of ice and snow
who run through our forests and mountains,
loud and terrible ghosts
whose names still resonate
during blizzard nights.
His eyes are fixed on her,
his face is a movie screen
of passing images.
He is six year old, his name is Lee.
they have the same gray eyes,
luminescent as winter.
I watch them in silence
I, too, like barbarians and lost cities

when they are here.

I walk along the coast,
the islands float on the horizon.

I pass by boys and girls,
teenagers, who smile at me
and wonder: who is this old man?

Their eyes speak for them!

Some almost touch me
and I can breathe their smell or rather
the smell of this summer afternoon sweat
on their skin.

I think of Lee, over there
far from summer and
far from the sweat of living skin

I think of Lee
far from the wind and far from the sea
dry under a ground foreign to him
and foreign to me.

I think of my son
who could be their father.

Sometimes the sun, a dirty orange,
a shadow thrown on the blue of the pond
the long silver thread of a scale
and these words, forever lost,
we would love to find again, childhood memories
sweet taste of apples
under the tongue of a kid lost
for so many years,
of a kid like me
who saw the cliffs
as a promise of journeys
in certitudes, elsewhere.

Elsewhere, we repeat to ourselves
day after day, night after night.
But, we are never elsewhere.
We are here! Always here!
Trapped in ourselves
between life and death
until nothing comes.

Crossing the border.
Coming back!
Returning to the child
Catriona's smile
Hearing her laugh
through the open window
Telling myself summer will come back
just to say something
just to speak to myself
Crossing the border
one more time
one last time
telling myself she will be there.

Lobster Fishing

It took weeks to repair the traps
and pots,
bruising our fingers, scraping
our palms on the belly of night
in the fold of the rocks,
foam on our lips
foam on the waves
our blood coming and going like
the ebb and flow of the ocean.
Far away, I see an island,
perhaps Mount Desert Island!
I don't know anymore.
The swell rocks me and torments me.
Blended smell of petrol, pitch and vomit,
our boat heaves.
Ropes burn our gloves and
flay the skin, and
salt adds its own dose of searing.
If lobsters have a sense of humor,
no doubt they are laughing at us.

Walking for eight days with the bare minimum
a backpack on my shoulders
sleeping under the leaves.
The earth is welcoming,
it takes the shape of the body, of its flaws
and of its dreams.
Finally coming back to find the forest,
the silence sleeping around the house
before the first chase of the small quarry
and their predators
before the night
before the tarnished spark of stars dying
with no one caring.

I remember the freezing cold
of that autumn day.
Death at my side
under the white sheet, under the blanket
her body hard and dry like floating wood.
I did not see her body
but I could feel it.
Only her face on the pillow,
I looked at her and I knew.
I could have named her!
And I think I did.
I gave death a name.
And since that day
every single day I walk with her
every single day my memory holds her hand.

Tonight I miss the sea,
the black and gray sea of my childhood,
a sea watched by northern gannets
and sorrow,
crisscrossed by a myriad of fish
without names.
Not a single noise pierces the wood, not a single rumor…
my eyes, then, turn to the sky
look for the beam of the light house
while counting the constellations.
Suddenly a shooting star,
a flying fish,
a vivid crack in the width of the world
a line of foam on the rocks of night.

To walk alone
to look at the landscape without recognizing a thing;
to know nothing anymore, to even stop expecting
when suddenly the knock of a woodpecker on a trunk
the shrill scream of an osprey
the flashing spark of a trout
cutting a river
the name of which you have forgotten

and suddenly you are not alone
the world surrounds you, cuddles you
like a mother her child

and in spite of the wrinkles that now
mark you
you surprise yourself
to find it all good.

The house is getting emptier and emptier
my words echo
little by little even the shadows retreat
the forest folds
on the weariness of the oil lamp.
The last traces of deer
have dried on the trail's hide,
like tattoos of the past.
Their last caresses on the tree trunks
resemble very ancient wrinkles,
blackened scars in the bark
deep and fragile.
They tell us a story
that will never return,
a lost love, a heap of sorrow.
I bend with pain,
my fingers brush a tuft of hair
left on the forest floor
mingled with the carpet of dead leaves,
I do not dare to pick it up, to take it in my hand,

I, too, am only fleeting.

Tomorrow again
night will follow day
it will be longer

the night is always longer
the lamp on the table
cuts through the shadows

like the wrinkles on my face
a little farther
always a little
farther
from my eyes
and the gray they bear.

The whiteness of snow, of frost,
inside!
I mean,
"the cold inside me!"
Since when is it my master
my steward and my keeper?
For how many years,
in me, this emptiness?
An envelope that would no longer hold anything
no letter, no word of love,
not a single postcard
of a seaside resort,
of a sunset on unknown sand dunes,
of a shore when the cliffs have the colors of a storm.
Since the end of this afternoon in May 74
in the clear warmth of spring?
Two years later, on an early autumn morning?
Or two seconds ago?

It does not matter!
Time, as a whole
fits in the first second
repeated until eternity.
My life like my death
will be the same emptiness.
Only the cold remains, no matter the season.

The Forgotten

Life, sometimes, lets itself be forgotten
between two screams of birds
in the bottom of a paper basket
on a crumpled paper
holding a few words of love
or hate.
Life lets itself be forgotten
in all the words we do not say
all the silences we cultivate
like dry
everlasting flowers.
We only look at it
passing by.
We forget it, we forget ourselves—
corpse lying on an autopsy table.

Some nights I say aloud the name of Eastborough,
the name of my early childhood.
No image comes to me—
I mean no precise memory,
too faded, these pictures that never existed—
simply smells,
the smell of fish my father brought back with him
on pay day.
The smell of the sea, so different from the smell of the ocean,
and the scent of my mother
light as chalk dust.
Some nights I go back there
although I know
death is immovable.

I walked for a long time in the snow,
the night had brought it to us in silence.
the air is light,
the wind, now gone, has left some traces.
It squeaks under the soles of my boots.
I have been walking alone here for years,
even my dog has gone.
Attacked by a bigger and stronger animal
he fought for a long time.
I would not have had his courage
or tenacity.
It was a morning like this one,
red on snow.

The wild geese are back
this morning they flew by, triumphant,
above the house
their beaks filled with cackles.
Each year I wait, impatient, for their return
as I wait for spring:
the tender green, the softer brown
of trees under the light.
The V of their flight
announcing the spring on the mirrored sky:
reflections of lakes, of shivering trout.
I followed them until my neck hurt.
They were going toward Lake Champlain.
Did they fly above Mount Katahdin?
These migrating travelers,
do they remember their first feathers,
the egg that brought them to the world,
the precise place where, perhaps, they go back?...
Suddenly, I imagine the whiteness of the fox,
the honey eyes of the bear after sleep:

a hint of shame
blends with the joy of their return.

For almost half of a century
I have lived far from Sussex
at the edge of forests
in the intimacy of the conifers
and their needles
their emerald green shining on snow
or in the depth of their shade
at the heart of the solstice.
For almost fifty years
I have been looking for the child
I remember.

My poem is a space
of a small surface.
It fits in the sound of splitting wood
in a bird stepping
on dry leaves.
Sometimes, only
the flight of an eagle
makes it soar.

Strange soul my soul
just a step from the mystery
at the edge of sorrow
looking in the distance
at the blue coast of Maine.

I too
have a pocket mirror.

Yesterday, dead drunk!
I spent a long time
talking to the Indian at the drugstore
before noticing that
the red man's paint
was peeling from his wooden face.
The sheriff, kindly, left me alone
he knows I had been married
that my son was a hero, not a veteran
he knows I live among the sounds of the forest
where I know all the animals,
half trapper, half hobo,
he does not know my name!
This morning, hungover,
drums dancing under my skull
and tears in my eyes.
The sun is red,
I have to ask
why heroes
are often the dead
whose names are forgotten.

Death waits for me,
I observe her and she watches me
The sole difference between us
The intensity in the look

This poem is the last one written by Robert Nash before he disappeared on May 31, 1995.

Poems to a
French Friend

To you my friend I speak of my son.
To whom could I say that I miss him?

To you my friend I speak of my son
as an ocean lies between us,
and so many waves like tears

rain pouring on your windows, over there,
in Brittany, on the gray granite shores
swollen skin after sorrow.

To you my friend I speak of my son
because I know you are listening!

Saint-Paul Island

Catriona told me "I am Saint-Paul Island
the hospital, the cemetery
I bear it all in me
as I carried our son.
My eyes are the whole strait,
the gray water and the winter ice".

I did not know what to say.
My words, even simple ones,
frozen in the salt of her tears

still, escaping me tonight
as I write to you.
They resemble a skiff
taking to sea and getting lost.
They are the salmon
that cannot spawn and die
caught up in the rafts of logs
going down our rivers.

I am mute.
Behind the window, the wind quiets down.
The earth has already forgotten
and there is nothing I can do.

My friend, this is not a letter—
I could not write one—

this is not even a poem
just a shipwreck, one more on the river.

Tonight, Catriona and I are Saint-Paul Island.

1974

That day the sun crashed.
Winter came in June
cold split the wood of our house
together with our hearts.
Our hands cracked
Our eyes crackled
as leaves in a fire.

That day,
I found stars slumped on the rocking chair,
stunted stars, cold fires,
a cosmos dying with hardly any ash.

A letterhead
Crumpled by a trembling hand,
an ever-trembling hand.

It is written that your family now has a hero.
But you no longer have a family.

Sometimes, when pain and sorrow are too heavy
when sadness lines my eyes,
I return to Hayange.
I see our youth passing by on old scooters,
both of us rootless
free and frightened.
It was the end of the war, the beginning of the fifties
you, teaching me useful words
me telling you my America
the one I knew and where, you said,
you would never go.
You were always a man of his word!
Both of us looking at the sweet girls
passing by in the street.

When the pain stretches and hums in Catriona
when sadness and anger suffocate me
I return to the foot of the blast-furnaces,
near you my friend
to the heat of the steel,
the seep of the flowing metal
calms me.

A few days in Delaware
walking on the Delmarva peninsula
and the woods of the First State
Catriona is happy
trees soothe her.
I often carry our two backpacks
her smile lightens them
on my shoulders
the light falling from branches
dresses her in tender green.
She is beautiful
I wait for her, she listens to the sounds of the invisible,
trying to recognize the animals hiding in it.
Life is there, everywhere,
today, walking with us.

Tonight, pain
is fully present
it runs through the house like a shiver
the modulation of cries
up and down the wooden stairs
makes the steps squeak.
Impossible to sleep in our bed,
to sleep near her.
In the kitchen, I drink a beer.
Not to get drunk,
just to hold on to a simple act,
to life.
Outside, the night is quiet
through the window the North Star winks at me.

The day falls fast,
shadows lengthening
merging with the night.
Darkness hardens,
onyx stone, ebony wood.
No more noises outside,
no barking dogs
nor mewing cats.
The neighbors'cars
are neatly parked along the sidewalk
or in their garages

all is dead

Catriona sleeps.

Again, I read Lee's letters,
the letters he sent from Đà Lạt.
No complaints, ever.
He spoke to his mother,
of landscapes so different from ours,
of children's faces coming down the mountains,
all so beautiful but hiding sometimes a danger
present in the silence between his words
but unimaginable and unbearable to us.

I read the letters of our son, again
Catriona is upstairs.
The doctor came by this morning
She will no longer go to the hospital, there is no point.
I re-read the letters
I read them, slowly
and dried tears
prevent new tears from coming.

This morning, once again
I finished the book—
The one we read together
on the eastern border.
This was our youth
"a season like another," you said.

I would stumble in a language that was not mine
a language I borrowed from you
and, you, for fun, would layer in
what I later learned to be *argot**.

I was, without knowing it,
a poor Argonaut
with no fleece

as we raised our beers
to our next travels.

*French slang

Catriona has no more words
she is an immense silence
her body, her arms around me
are a silence
a silence within my own silence
our tears are a silence
and our silences fit in one of our tears

we no longer know which one
they all resemble one another

they all have the same name
like an insect that will not fly

the same name
I keep in my throat
and Catriona keeps safe
in her belly

as I write these words to you, my friend.

Discovering the world.
Traveling! Going from country to country
measuring ourselves against the sequoias
and not being astonished
following a tornado on the horizon
and praying that nothing changes
hunting alligators
and marveling at the color of the bayou
trapping bears
and shouting at the mountain
simply to see
where the echo lands
doing all that and much more
before the end

as everybody else.

I affirm:
a worm
is much more powerful
than the A-bomb

Go figure it out
if you can

if you want.

Catriona did not sleep at all
this morning she is agitated.
A fever, maybe.
At first I did not understand and then...
the radio in the kitchen!
I no longer know why I had turned up the volume
a baseball match, a concerto,
or news from the world?
I no longer know!
An April morning, I made myself coffee,
scalding.
Tornados have crossed the border but
in the garden nothing has changed
Lee's swing
creaks in the wind.

To go up North
nothing holds me here
cemeteries are the same everywhere
and the chest contains only one heart.

What holds me warm is in me
what makes me cold is in me

Now everything belongs to me
since I have nothing left.

Sometimes I want to go away
back to the Youth
we did not pay attention to
and wasted
because we were just what she told us to be
carefree and confident young men,
convinced she was an everlasting
eternal Uroboros
the constant rebirth of a deep and
endless river
where we would bathe from dusk to dawn.

We were wrong my friend
and you know it as much as I do.
We were wrong to believe only in ourselves
and if by any chance
we doubted ourselves
we were even more wrong.

The house has lost the scent of spring,
something heavy inhabits it.
The wind does not enter
even with the windows wide open.
Snow and summer rains
have become empty words.
It is no longer the house of a man and a woman,
It is a place to die
It is a dwelling
where our lives slowly burn
day after day
like the torment of water on dry earth.
It slides, washes and strips,
but never penetrates.
Every day is the same day, my friend
we have become that day
and we will remain in it
regardless of the other days,
all the other days
since this summer afternoon, in 1974

Some days, unexpectedly,
when I come into our bedroom,
Catriona—the woman I loved, the woman I love—
is there.
I see her clear eyes,
just lightly faded, slightly tired,
her delicate face, paler,
her hair, the color of the Phoenix, thinner.
She smiles at me, she speaks to me about life, about
the birds she hears, outside, in the garden.
Surprising me because I don't hear them anymore.
She reaches her hand to me, and I give her mine
I reach my hand to her, and she gives me hers.
Tomorrow, she will find the strength,
we will go out to the porch.
She closes her eyes

Turn down the light as you leave! she tells me.

They kiss!
Perhaps he shows her the pictures
he took just before
the last!
Perhaps, she talks to him about me,
telling him I am getting old
and will continue to get older
before we are reunited.
She smiles as she tells him
that I have put on some weight
but that I do watch it, that I walk!
He says he is happy to see her.
He says he remembers me
as I was the day he left.

I cannot speak to them
They don't hear me
even when I scream, especially when I scream
so, I cry, sometimes,
silently.

I spent the night reading Blaise Cendrars
—the book you sent me long ago.
Some words escape me
but the pages, one by one, take me away.
far from the silence of illness
far from its screams and suffering.
Far, also, from the dog
yapping, fearful, at my legs
as if feeling a danger coming toward us,
a tornado or something else I do not want to name.
I stayed at Catriona's side,
until she fell
prisoner of a whirling sleep.
Then, I drank a glass of wine before opening this book
in which Blaise speaks of elsewhere.

I wanted to make a friend.

Catriona speaks to me about Maine.
She tells me she would love to live there
and, perhaps die in Vermont.
She smiles at me, but her face does not light up.
There is almost no light left in her.
Her complexion is waxy
her hands, her whole body
has slowly lost its flesh.
She is so thin that the word itself
has no more meaning to me.
We share our silences,
we feel good like this, still together!

Our eyes speak for us.

Leaving for Maine
getting closer to the border, to the ocean
throwing a stone far in front of me,
this stone, a goal,
a world to reach.

Onward!

Picking up the stone
and throwing it again
as far as possible
reaching another world

which, I know, will be the same.

Leaving for Maine.

Backpack

A backpack
nothing else for a life
a few childhood memories
a beach, perhaps, on the coast of England
a father, a mother
who divines what you will become
and time passing
flocks of clouds
storms
sun breaks
moments of happiness
the ring she slides on your finger.
Sorrow!
the moment someone asks
if you want to remove it from her finger.
Silence
shovels of earth
clatter on plain wood.
Pictures found
then put away.
A backpack for what is left.

Flashes, at times,
a spring afternoon
a summer evening
her eyes, her mouth
a fall morning
in the Laurentians
the spark of her smile
just a little sad
the depth
of our winter nights
and old age settling
as a sharing

her name, finally, always…
She was of all my seasons.

Alone!
A strange word.
A word we can never fully grasp.
A word which resonates less
than the word loneliness.
A word that weighs on me only
when I write to you, my friend;
when I try, through my writing, to express it to you
and to explain it to myself,
but I can neither express
nor explain it!
So, I squeeze the paper into a ball
and I throw it on the wood floor
feeling only
a little more alone.

For a long time I walked in Augusta's streets
a stranger here more than anywhere else.
In my ear Catriona's voice.
In my hand the memory of hers.
Around me noises of cars,
The buzz of construction sites, jackhammers,
and animated conversations of students
going to their classes.
I see our bedroom
Catriona's body, a shadow under the sheet,
Telling me of her desire to live or to die in Maine,
remembering stories from her childhood,
stories her father told her.
Books read together
after prayers and before dreams.
Books filled with rain song and war cries
Of the Abenaki tribes.
Augusta, today, is filled with other noises
and Catriona is only a silence
in the wild beat of my heart.

I have been working for four months
the house is small
but large enough for me
if I want to wait here for winter.
The man in the hardware store knows me now.
He thinks I am crazy
but is reassured by my credit card.
One day he asked
why I had bought that shack in the forest.
I told him it was
to better know the trees.
Today the trees
are my only companions
except the old badger
I have never seen
but who leaves his tracks
pressed in the earth.

Kennebec River

I went down to the river.
I tried to imagine it during the time of the trappers
covered with fur like a dancer,
or a prostitute wrapped in pelts
of river otter, raccoon or bear—
Half-socialite extravagantly dressed
in violence and beauty—
flowing and swaying peacefully
assured of herself
and of the depth of her bed.

I tried to imagine her as a source
pure and limpid, unsure perhaps,
just before leaving Moosehead Lake
heading for her dissolute life.

I could not.

Life passed by,
time has spun on itself
before lying down
like a restless dog.
I spent the week
building the porch
—three steps, rough wood.
I am my unique apprentice
I am learning how to become
what I am becoming.

Yesterday I saw the badger for the first time.
He lives under the house
unless it is I
who lives above his burrow?
The question remains unanswered.
I have named him Emerson.

Who knows why!

Starting all over.
But can we ever?
Starting everything again
but when we turn back
we can never retake
the steps we took.
Each step backward
can never be the exact same step
only a new step.
I am here, elsewhere
but still the same,
just a little older, a little more pessimistic
a little more alone, my friend,
afraid like a lamb under thunder,
clinging, like a mountain climber to his axe,
to what you call my poems
so as to not lose my grip
and crash on my sorrow.

Walking everyday a little farther
In the depth of fall.
this morning, I listen but don't yet hear
the scream of an osprey
or the silky rustling
of small rodents around the house.
Last night, big fuss
Emerson is upset
though we live as friendly neighbors.
This morning on the footsteps of the porch
the remains of three mice crunched
under the sole of my shoe.

Nights are longer and longer.
Can you understand my friend?
I push my body
until I don't recognize it
until I exhaust it, hate it.
Sometimes I think I hear
my muscles grind
but it is only the wind in the trees.

Here, humans live in silence.
Only animals speak sometimes.
I do as they do
to be accepted
to belong
to exist only through their eyes.
Solitude wraps me
—a big wool sweater
keeping me warm.
The steam rising
from my scalding coffee
is my only true travel.

Gray Bear stopped by this morning,
he was going hunting.
He was heading north.
"I am going hunting" he said to me.
He was dressed in his full regalia
sumptuous clothes as old as he, as worn.
Only his rifle was new.
When I told him
he had no cartridges
he simply replied
"Youth can't be hunted
we ought to track its memory."
We drank a strong coffee
Then I watched him leave

He did not look back.

Surprise!
I collected wild honey
the last of the year
bees are already falling asleep.
The forest is red.
Tomorrow the moon, color of dried blood,
will highlight the shadows.
There will be stillness between the trees.
Animals will take cover.
I brought in wood for the fire

I don't really know why.

The world is beside itself—
tiny noises, cracking sounds of twigs,
sucking sound the water in ditches
the blue of the snow
weighing heavily on the pines.
I care about all these little things
that paint my days
dressing them in flesh
and color.
I simply follow with my eyes
the shiver of a quarry
passing through the undergrowth
unaware.

Catriona is with me.
She inhabits the whole house!
I am in the memory of her body,
inside.
I talk to her about Lee
I try to imagine what kind man
he would be today
if he would resemble her
if he would love this place
where even "nowhere" has no meaning.

Night comes with silence
and questions.

Nobody stops by anymore
except Gray Bear and a few of his kind
when night or pain surprise them
half-way in their nowhere
We understand each other!
I talk about the few sounds that surround me,
they know how to listen.
We often speak
words of silence,
parting only at dawn
holding hands
offering each other a treasure.

Last night, big fuss under the house
Emerson is upset.
And this morning fuss in the kitchen
Emerson is looking for fruit
he can't find.
I promise to buy some in Augusta.

This afternoon
two snouts
peek out of the burrow

I feel less alone.

With twilight comes the first scream of tawny owls.
The wind is down.
Between the trees, orange pools
tell me of the sun's silent fire.
Gray wolf told me
It was the gods falling asleep.
after having written the law of the universe.
I believe in nothing anymore
especially not God!
I think of the Weymouth pine.
Does the tawny owl nest there?
Her cry is to me
a thread stretched over the world.

In a bookstore in Augusta, I found
Les forêts du Maine de Thoreau.*
I read it as you drink hard liquor,
in one shot.
Strange feeling to have entered the book.
Of course no cedars here
but the same kind of ghosts, rooted.
Secular trees trembling in me.
I call to them.
I want to follow his footsteps to Quakish Lake.
A ten-day hike
to wash the past
and finally sift through it
keeping only the gold of late evening
when the forest falls asleep with my pain.

*The Maine Woods, *by Henry David Thoreau*

Trees shed their water all night
and all day.
On the ground, cracks then clefts,
the earth is aging.
Under the house, the burrow is empty
no letter from Emerson
only tracks in the mud.
This morning the sky is washed
almost white
leaves of many shades and
sounds of startled squirrels move in branches.

This is already a lot.

Nothing else here
only myself
—the emptiness of a body
estranged from itself
in the depths of winter

I envy the spruce trees.

Poems Gathered
in a Green Folder

I move farther and farther
away from myself
keeping the memory
of a mountain,
a badger's profile,
the bright new green
of a forest of firs
and the memory of a woman: Catriona
her memory there
in the weight of a cry.
Not enough
or too much
to simply hold on.

Sometimes I call her
and sometimes she responds.
I sit on the steps
holding a beer
waiting for twilight to come
that precise moment
when everything shifts
—the death of day
never buried.

Sometimes I don't remember
I don't want to remember anymore!
So, I invent another life,
other places,
where we are together.
Lee has grown older,
his sons run in a blue garden
—in the glinting light of spruce—
his daughters listen to Catriona
telling stories of a far-away country
or of Saint Paul Island
while I smoke this heavy tobacco
I never even liked.

I walk with her.
Her weight in my heart
heavier than the backpack on my shoulders.
We walk for days and days
at night we sleep in the open
(nothing unusual)
yet, only my shadow
is elongated
by the campfire's flames.
So, I stand up and call to her:
"We are in Maine,
you and I, together!"
Always a bird responds
the very same bird perhaps.

Here again, I write to you my dear Robert*
to talk about me
the man I no longer am
or perhaps never was.
Again, I write to you my friend
because I heard you have been sick.
You said nothing in your letters!
I write to you so as to not break our thread
to not yet give in
to what awaits us all.
Your letter of June 24th
is an encouragement.
You write:
like Goethe, always more light.
The friendship we have shared for so many years
lightens the darkest of our words
the heaviest of our movements
and all the silences lingering between us
crackle like burning pine.

*Strangely enough, the name of Jean-Claude's father was also Robert. Thus, the two friends had the same first name.

Dusk falls, dark.
Does it add
darkness to the night
when it flows and gathers
at the tops of the trees
at the height of their branches
thickening like a humor.
I have always loved
the ambiguity of language
reminiscent of my youth.
And even more tonight
as I stand, alone,
facing the silence of trees.
A moth
wagers her life
against the lightbulb swaying in the wind.

Trying to reason with her perhaps …

Sitting on the steps
I drink a beer with Randall.
He came to fix my Valiant.
I don't use it anymore
but who knows . . .
Between two sips
we talk about the passing of time.
I believe the very same leaves
grow back each year
on the same trees.
Of course, I say nothing.
He would think I am crazy
would blame my solitude.
So, I simply nod
as I down the rest of my beer.

Yesterday, great surprise
when I realized
that in French the same word means
both an old mountain range
and a flower bed
Massif.
Today
the world is different
I see the tiniest pebble
as a bouquet
and every single thought
before my eyes
takes the shape of a lofty peak.

How long has it been
since I went to town?
Supplies are running out
and books, too
—their backs broken
their pages dog-eared
and my hand calloused.
I read once more
Carver's poems.
I like his simple
everyday words
hiding other things
as life does.

The northern wind stings my eyes.
Winter is coming!
A sun, ever more orange,
dives each evening under the horizon.
Yesterday, I hacked a dead tree,
stripped the bark.
A sharp sound, then, the air sliding
before the shock, the earth,
in the compact silence of the woods.
The first snow will come soon
with perhaps, one day,
sketched on it
the tracks of an artic hare
or, if luck holds, the flight of a snowy owl.

This morning, less than three hundred feet from the house,
on the trunk of an old fir,
claw marks.
A bear marked its territory.
Considering the height
and depth of the scratches in the bark
it must have been a fully grown male
five feet and more than two hundred pounds
and so much silence all around.

Beautiful guardian angel.

The first snow.
In all this white,
trunks blacken
as if the color
were tightening
concentrating
inside the wood veins
in mine too
to better resist.

Why did I think, then,
that death would be solid?

Last night, I dreamed of Jacques.
Do you remember him, Robert,
and the casting flow which took him
there, in Hayangue, in 1959?
Sometimes, I still see him
falling into the liquid fire.
He falls from the footbridge
and I fall with him
and you fall with us
and with us our youth
the one we shared all three.
We fall endlessly!
Our twenties swirling in the flow.
I wake-up with a start,
older than I would have thought,
more alone than I would like
and something tells me
it is irretrievable.

Last week I found
Catriona's book on her bedside
—the one she was reading when we were still in Delaware—
The Maine Woods by Henry Thoreau.
My hands trembled
yet, I was walking within the pages
filling my lungs with fresh air
and memories.
I was even expecting Thoreau at my door
and together we would have walked
and breathed side by side
even if his woods were not mine.
In the evening, Blue Bear helped me
with Algonquian words.
Listening to the words
I entered more deeply
into the bodies of the trees
the thickness of the sky and earth
feeling even more the presence of the living.
Animals looking at me for who I am,
then, quickly, looking away
so as not to disturb me.
The next second
they are one with the green
and all the many other colors
in which the woods move, pulse, grow.

Climbing the Appalachian trail
to the sharp ridge, until
the blade.
Trying to see Mount Katahdin
as Thoreau did.
Going through the woods, then the rocks,
the heavy shadow of granite.
Earning the valley as a moment of rest
the eyes lingering there so the body can pause
before moving onto the cliff, the precipice,
where it could lose its balance.
A misstep awaits
me, a faltering acrobat on the sharp string of stones,
a little man, so tiny, approaching Mount Baxter.

I am back after twenty days of hiking,
my body is tired, my words dry, burnt
by my saliva, by the salt of my sweat
walking alone for so long.
More than 300 hundred miles round trip
with on my back this "too much"
we call "the minimum",
but I saw the highest mountain
as the Penobscot call her.
She felt my weight on her stone skin
we got closer, we bonded,
we recognized each other perhaps.
I left her a piece of my strength
and she gave me her beauty
we are even!

I see Cape Neddick, the lighthouse,
the light on the ocean
and the noises of the world, still there despite everything.
It was the end of 1979
The president had just refused to extradite the Shah
I was holding Catriona's hand
small in mine.
We did not care about the Shah
we were walking, the light on our back
as always.
I felt Catriona's hand stiffen in mine
I held it a bit tighter,
a tear rolled down her cheek.
I said nothing, I clenched my teeth,
trying to believe
it was because of the scenery.

When I look around
my gaze does not get lost.
My years have seen so many people
fade away, and so many things.
Space has grown around me
emptiness has taken its place
all of it.
A few books on my bookshelf
still keep me company
Thoreau, Carver, Emerson
and as many French authors.
Close to my bed a picture
Catriona is smiling
she holds Lee in her arms.
Time makes no sound
only the door sometimes squeaks.

Last night, I dreamed of river otters
I was swimming with them
feeling light.
We were fishing for wild oysters
and pink clams in the river...
They were showing me how!
I knew it was absurd,
but I was happy
as I had not been for a long time.
So, I became active
my sweat flowing into the river
raising its level.
When I told my dream to the Indian
he was not surprised.
He looked at me in silence
before telling me
that the river otter was the eleventh totem,
a point of equilibrium between freedom
and maternal love,
that Catriona had come back
to tell me that she was free now
she was with Lee
and they were both protecting me.

Why did I simply want to believe . . .

A smell of wood against the wall
a smell of sap and resin
creeps into the house.
The first blizzards
have already passed
and looking for tracks is becoming more difficult.
Animals, too, shelter from the cold
entering their holes
shutting the openings
burrowing under the leaves.
Woodpeckers do not drum on the trunks anymore.
Everyone enters the woods, the forest.
A smell of wood creeps into the house
a smell of dry sap and resin.
Why did I think
of the smell of death?

My nights are becoming more and more difficult
the river otters come less and less often.
The fire's flames reflect and hold the shadows
of everything around me.
I do not switch the light on anymore
—electricity is a cold sun.
At night I prefer the oscillations of candles.
Their glow
holding shadows
without disclosing them
feeds my sleeplessness.
Forms move
the world dissolves,
fragments, a spark in my memory
tries to remember the passing of the day.
Outside a sound, a quiver
the hoot of an owl.

Life, still.

Yesterday morning a fox in one of the traps.
Which one of us is the most surprised?
How long has he been there
with his back leg snared?
I approach.
My thigh hurts.
He recoils,
shows his fangs, then yelps.
He is afraid, he hurts.
I know it well
we are not that different.

I see that he has tried to free himself
his leg is an open wound.
The bone is visible.

Tonight, the fox is in the shed.
I took care of him, wrapped a bandage around his leg.
The poultice of moss and berries
should work.

It has been five days since the axe slipped.
Tonight, the pain is excruciating.
I clench my teeth. It hurts.
I should go to town
to see a doctor
but the Plymouth refuses to start.

The fox is back to his habits
and I, I avoided the worst.

"Gangrene, septicemia," said the doctor.
Blue Bear, the Indian, took me in his pickup.
Apparently, I had a fever and was delirious
when he found me.
I just remember the pain
with each bump on the dirt road
until we reached the asphalt.

I start walking again, little by little
I return to myself
limping on my crutch.

Blue Bear stops by
with fish.
He says he is sharing
but I think he goes fishing just for me.
With nightfall, sometimes the fox points his nose
through the door which I never fully close.
A sign of friendship.

Perhaps I just imagine it.

Here comes the half-season
with its shades of green
that the wind rustles
and brightens.
Sometimes a moving shadow
hangs on it
animals, too, pause at the start of a trail.
Oh, to stay there, buried in the thickness
and commotion of trees . . .

I would like to write about something else,
of life, of streets,
of everyday hustle and bustle
and the beauty of women, I don't even know.
I would like to describe the laugh of a child
and a second after
the burst of tears, the sobbing
and whispered words of love
made of tenderness.

I would like so much to write
about all this, but I can't.
So, I stare at the sun
pierced by the needles of the pines
as it streams through the branches
and I tell myself:

tomorrow, perhaps.

Here, alone,
too often alone,
with my only companion
a badger as solitary
as me.

A badger I barely know
and who
most of the time
completely ignores me.

For sure, he and I miss
Babel and its tower

Because, since then,
words have disappeared.
Between him and me words are dying
for not being used.

I think I have lost one more word
this morning

Home sweet home!

The Letter

Sometimes, rarely I must say,
you speak about your wife
and children whom I don't know.
Your daughter, your son
you tell me of their teenage life
their little lies and mischief
life hanging to the day
as laundry drying on the line.

you speak of them
quietly
so as not to hurt me.

But, do you know that in fact
It brings me back to life.
I can see Catriona, Lee, and me together
and we can be for a moment with you all
my friend.
The ocean between us
fits entirely in the blue flow
of ink on the page.
My eyes follow the meandering stream
in its down-stokes and upstrokes
until the silent abyss of the final point.

Until my solitude comes back
with the December cold all around.

Almost two full days
without moving.
The wind is blowing
outside the window
yet, the treetops are still.
I am out of beer!
Blue Bear brought me some dry fish,
nuts and maple water.
I have nothing to offer him,
so, we talk of the coming of spring.

"Each human life is a mystery"
So begins a poem by Carver.
The line swirls in me.
Yes, "in me!"

Perhaps because of the silence
that fills me
to the brim
as the earth fills a grave
shovel by shovel

I hear the line grumbling
in my belly,
stomach noises on crappy days.

"Each human life is a mystery"
getting harder to decipher.

"You speak with your eyes
you know how to look at things
see what the wind brings to the trees,
the hesitations of the badger near the river
and of the river when the weight of night
slows her flow.
You know how to listen to the grass in the meadow
what the pebbles say under our steps
and the hidden meaning
of a screeching eagle's flight.
You are not alone!
You are one of us
the badger welcomes you as one of them.
Since you are doing something else with your anger
your eyes speak more than your mouth"

This is what the Indian told me yesterday.
I have not yet fully understood.
I finish reading *The Birth-Mark* *
close the book and turn off the light.
The night slips under the door
tired of bumping against the window.
I stay here, seated, still.
The night is passing by
I gaze at the stars.

What else can I do
What better? ...

* *Short story by Nathaniel Hawthorne included
in* Mosses from an Old Manse *(1846)*

We invaded Grenada!
So many soldiers in such a small place
like an elephant
on a cherry.
My radio hisses
there is static on the line.
Screams, commands, cries, detonations
collateral damage
destruction, rubble
bodies left on the street.
Meanwhile
in the Oval Office
Ronald is getting briefed.
Through the window, if he is so inclined,
he would see the first leaves falling
on the lawns
swirling
before reaching the ground.

Gardeners already raking.

The Raccoon

I have a new friend,
he came one night, without warning.
No luggage, just himself
and the racket of the trash cans.
He came with a mask
helped by a moonless night
—drawn, perhaps,
by the smell of the crawfish I had eaten.
The next day,
my sleep being precious,
I leave a few nuts and a bowl of water
on my doorstep.
In the morning, all gone,
washed clean.

Now, I should invite myself to his place!

My body is betraying me
we disagree ever more often
and yet, we have shared the sun
the rain, the winds
and the smells of the forest in all seasons
even when time would stop in me
frozen in ice or in memories.
And yet, my body and I
have loved a woman
shared the thrill of the flesh
and thus, have loved
all women.
My body lent me its strength, its agility
I fed it with my emotions.
Then why this slower heart
this stiffer body
this drier soul
and this breath weaker with each small step
with the slightest elevation?

Sun reflected in the water of the tin basin
a star falling
straight from the sky.
The galvanized metal heats up,
yesterday the raccoon
left some fruit behind;
it swirls now
a gentle oscillation at the center
like an island on the ocean.

Little voyage
endless dream.

Self Portrait

After twenty years
more or less
around myself
nothing much has changed.
Trees have grown a little
their trunks have darkened, perhaps,
unless it is my eyes
that have clouded
or my perception
that has dimmed and faded.
Animals still come for a visit.
The same ones? Others?
This questioning
and the doubt it holds
pleases me,
gives me hope
while in the mirror
the wrinkles I see
all over my face
attest to the certainty of death.

Yesterday, I Saw Jean

Today, unexpectedly, I run into Jean
I think, at first, she did not recognize me
she hesitated
then, she just said my name: Robert
as if it were the most improbable thing
she could possibly say
in the parking lot
while she was putting groceries
into the trunk of her Pontiac.
Her voice had not changed
her body was the body of a woman.

I too hesitated
I did not know what to say
or how and when to stay silent
I kept seeing her
on Lee's arm
at the graduation ball.

What did we say?
I don't really remember.
Words
things said
about three decades ago
flood my memory
as clear
as if they had been said yesterday

by the same mouth
the same lips only with less makeup.

I simply heard she was married
to a stockbroker
living in Portland
had no children
and did not want any.

I did not dare to ask why?

On the way back
listening to *Green Grow the Lilacs* *
I was so mad at myself
for not having said a word.

Why did I stay more silent
than the wooden Indian at the drugstore?
Jean had nothing to do with it
she was simply alive
happy and alive
simply putting
her every-day life
in the trunk of her car
along with a bit of love and a bit of sorrow too, no doubt.
All that goes into
the days coming before and after
night.

Song by Harry Bellafonte

Sometimes, fatigue takes me.
My body gone,
as if I were not here anymore
I mean
not in this world.
For how long?
How many years
which seemed to me like seconds?
Time flows like a river
always carrying the same water.
I am at the center
my feet steady in the flow
of my memories
the bed is empty
no movement, not a single silvery fish.
In the house silence wraps everything
I am this silence and nothing else.

Outside the trees are still,
the wind has died.

I spent the morning following a column
of ants.
Though there was plenty to do!
Empty bottles of beer to toss,
dirty dishes in the sink,
letters to write, often not even sent.
And yet, I stay there, watching the ants,
their long march at the bottom of the porch.
Their number is infinite.
I follow them with my eyes,
they all look alike.
How far will I go in their company?
—I, who have stopped looking like myself long ago—
Are they finally going to see me,
accept me?

Halloween

Yesterday, it was All Saints Eve.
I have not seen one yet!
Gusts of wind were blowing against the windows
and I thought I heard: "Trick or treat"
but no child was running around.
It was *"oìche Shamhna"*
my grandfather's stories
my mother's fears.
I spent the day reading *Such Is My Beloved*
by Morley Callaghan.
At nightfall
my friend Jack Brent stopped by.
I saw the pick-up's headlights in the window.
He opened the door, laughing and bellowing
"Bourbon or treat"
I sliced some dried meat
took out two glasses
he opened his bottle of bourbon.

We laughed,
ate and drank.

CPSIA information can be obtained
at www.ICGtesting.com
Printed in the USA
BVHW030925250322
631887BV00009B/1